CHICKEN IN THE KITCHEN

Neal Zetter's Greatest Hits

troika

Published by TROIKA

First published in 2025

Troika Books Ltd,

Well House, Green Lane, Ardleigh, Colchester, Essex, CO7 7PD, UK

www.troikabooks.com

Text copyright © Neal Zetter 2025

Illustrations copyright © Emily Ford 2025

Designed and typeset by Wendy Mach (White Stone Pages)

The moral rights of the author and illustrator have been asserted

All rights reserved

A CIP catalogue record for this book is available

from the British Library

ISBN 978-1-912745-41-8

Printed in Poland by Totem.com.pl

CHICKEN IN THE KITCHEN

Neal Zetter's Greatest Hits

Illustrations by Emily Ford

troika

Contents

Bees in My Bananas

Ba nana nana nana nana nana nana nana nana
nana nana nana nana nana 8

I'm a Bee 10

Mr Onomatopoeia 12

Friday is Chip Day! 14

The Day My Underwear Went BOOM! 16

My Teacher's Got Eyes in the Back of Her Head . .18

The Detention Rap 20

Cool Addiction .22

It's Not Fine to Sit on a Porcupine

Fire Alarm 24

Have a Laugh .26

My Dad Thinks He's Cool 28

Match of the Day 30

When I am Prime Minister 32

Orangutan, utan, utan, utan, utan, utan 34

Mr Teacher is Our Teacher 36

Here Come the Superheroes

The Invisible Lady 38
My Superpower 40
Terrific Tot 42
Underneath the Mask 44

Yuck and Yum

Kids Love Ketchup 46
Pizza Delivery Man 48
My Secret Chocolate Stash 50
Claude le Croissant 52
Hot Stuff 54

Invasion of the Supervillains

The Rhyme Thief 56
Mwahahahaha! 58
Paintball 60

Gorilla Ballerina

Chicken in the Kitchen 62
Tarantula Down Your Toilet 64
We Want the Quagga! 66
I'm an Electric Eel 68
Animal Football Premiership Table 70

When the Bell Goes

Good Morning!. 72
Blah! Blah! Blah!. .74
Mum and Dad are Kissing Again 76
My Me-Only Zone .78
Fake News 80

Scared?

Haunted House. 82
I Don't Like Ssssssnakes 84
My Mummy is a Mummy 86
Something Down the Plughole 87
Scared?. 88

Bonus Poems

Things That Can't Fit in My Shoe 90
Just Be You 91

About the Poet. 92
About the Illustrator. 92
About this Collection 93

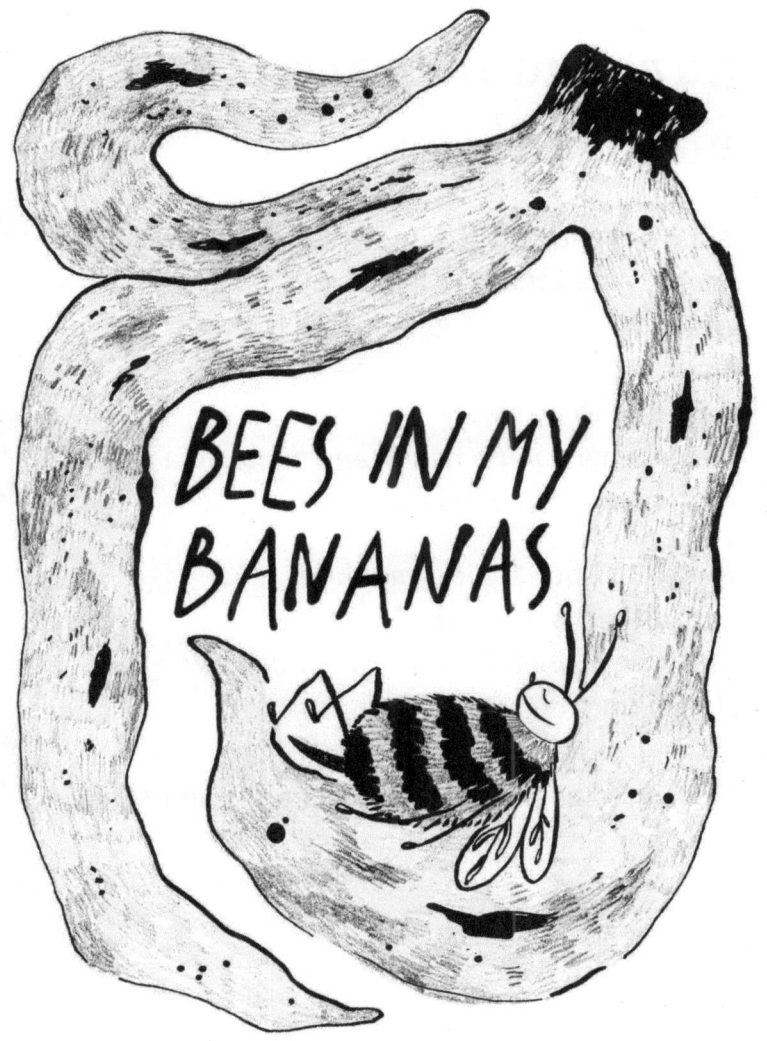

Ba nana nana nana nana nana nana nana nana nana nana nana nana nana nana

What's the longest fruit you've seen?
Found in milkshake, yoghurt and ice-cream
When they're on my plate, I lick it clean
A tremendous taste
Too good to waste
Ba nana nana nana nana nana nana nana nana
nana nana nana nana nana

You'll slip upon their slimy skin
So put the peel into the bin
What word doesn't stop once it begins?
Simply unending
I'm always bending my
Ba nana nana nana nana nana nana nana nana
nana nana nana nana nana

You can mash them
You can squash them
You can squish them
You can gulp them
You can fry them

You can spread them
You can pound them
You can pulp them
When I ask you what food you've had today
I'm hoping that you're going to say
Ba nana nana nana nana nana nana nana nana
nana nana nana nana nana

Monkeys eat them at the zoo
They're yellow and black, not orange and blue
Ideal in a soup or even a stew
They're versatile
Shaped like a smile
Ba nana nana nana nana nana nana nana nana
nana nana nana nana nana

Buy them by the kilo, pound or bunch
Stick them in your sandwich box for lunch
What's the ideal snack, when it comes to the crunch?
Travelling all the way from Jamaica
What fruit's got a name that's a record breaker?
Ba nana nana nana nana nana nana nana nana
nana nana nana nana nana

Before you get some from the store
Shout out this poem's title once more
Ba nana nana nana nana nana nana nana nana
nana nana nana nana nana

I'm a Bee

I'm a bee
I'm a bee
Buzzing round your head
Hear my sound all around
Like a very long zed
Not an A or a C
Or a D or an E
I'm a bee
I'm a bee
I'm a bee, bee, bee

I'm a bee
I'm a bee
Coloured yellow and black
I've got wings and a sting
So I might attack
My queen is the one
Who's a mum to me
I'm a bee
I'm a bee
I'm a bee, bee, bee

I'm a bee
I'm a bee
So loving that honey
Sit for hours on the flowers
In the summer when it's sunny

In my hive I survive
High up in a tree
I'm a bee
I'm a bee
I'm a bee, bee, bee

I'm a bee
I'm a bee
I'm a bee, bee, bee

I'm a bee
I'm a bee
I'm a bee, bee...bee!

Mr Onomatopoeia

I'm someone you'll want to know
Mr Onomatopoeia
Helping you spell every sound
That goes into your ears

Crocodiles I make them SNAP!
Windows I make SMASH!
Bees in springtime I make BUZZ!
Cars I make them CRASH!

I'm Mr Onomatopoeia
The SQUELCH in your wet welly
Though difficult enough to say
It's harder still to spell me

Ghosts and ghouls I make them WHOOOOOH!
Balloons I make them POP!
Chattering children I make SHUSH!
Rain I make DRIP, DROP! PLIP, PLOP!
DRIP, DROP! PLIP, PLOP!
DRIP, DROP! PLIP, PLOP!
Until the storm or shower stops

The loudest neighbour in your street
I cause fireworks to BOOM!
Write your noises like you hear them
And you'll top your class real soon

I make angry lions ROAR!
Big Ben I make him BONG!
Fingertips I make them CLICK!
Door bells I make DING-DONG!
DING-DONG!

I hope you're glad you met me
Mr Onomatopoeia
Helping you spell every sound
That goes into your ears

That goes into your ears
With onomatopoeia

Friday is Chip Day!

Friday is Chip Day
A love to lick your lips day
What do all our teachers say?
'Friday is Chip Day!'

Friday is a top day
The chips just never stop day
Not pork pie or lamb chop day
Friday is Chip Day!

Friday is a great day
No need to watch your weight day
A run to the school gate day
Friday is Chip Day!

Friday is the best day
A zip and zap and zest day
A plenty to digest day
Friday is Chip Day!

Friday is a cool day
A love to go to school day
An only just one rule day
Friday is Chip Day!

Friday is a fave day
A never misbehave day
An eat the food you crave day
Friday is Chip Day!

So grab vinegar, salt and tomato sauce
When that day comes around of course
If you're hungry enough to eat a horse
Don't worry 'cause...
Friday is Chip Day!

The Day My Underwear Went BOOM!

The day my underwear went BOOM!
Exploding like a burst balloon
The noise was heard upon the moon
The day my underwear went...

... POP!
Windows wobbled, ceilings rocked
I bought it from a classy shop
But still my underwear went...

... BANG!
Along my street the echoes rang
What happened? No one could explain
The day my underwear went...

... ZAP!
The cat leapt six foot off my lap
I got inspired to write this rap
The day my underwear went...

... BUST!
Vests vaporised, pants turned to dust
I heaved a sigh of deep disgust
The day my underwear went...

... BAM!
I was an underwearless man
With just a burnt thread in my hand
The day my underwear went...

... BOOM!
A choking smoke consumed my room
My normal life can't be resumed
Because my underwear went...

... BOOM!

My Teacher's Got Eyes in the Back of Her Head

My teacher's got eyes in the back of her head
So you'd better listen to what she said
She probably knows what you're doing
Even when you're in bed
If you mess about
Don't you know she'll catch you out?
It's one false move and you're dead

You're never out of her sights
So watch out where you tread
Where's my teacher got eyes?
In the back of her head

My teacher's got ears in strange places too
If someone talks in assembly, she always knows who
Last week she gave me detention because I spoke to you
If you say a word
Don't you know that you'll be heard?
But how she does it I haven't a clue

She's got X-ray vision
She'll fill you with dread
Where's my teacher got eyes?
In the back of her head

My teacher even knows when I'm telling lies
Perhaps she's employing an army of spies
I say 'Dog ate my homework, Miss' but she's too wise
When you tell a fib
Don't you know she'll know you did?
She'll say 'Stop telling porky pies!'

So don't mess with my teacher
Pick another instead
Where's my teacher got eyes?
In the back of her head

The Detention Rap

When school finished at half-past three
I didn't leave on time unfortunately
'Cause I messed around in history
Chemistry, biology and literacy
My teacher said I had to pay the penalty

I got a detention
I got a detention
Sir said I attract too much negative attention
If I attract any more, I'll receive a suspension
What did I get?
I got a detention

My punishment was writing many essays and lines
On how to show respect and listen all of the time
Concentrate on sharpening those ears of mine
What was the sentence imposed for my crime?

I got a detention
I got a detention
My timetable had an extra hour extension
You walked home while I walked in the other direction
What did I get?
I got a detention

I acted like the class clown and I got caught
Now I'm worried about what will be in my report
Though I pleaded like an innocent 'It wasn't my fault'
I was told it's a lesson that I had to be taught

I got a detention
I got a detention
I was going to be a prefect now I'm out of contention
If you see my Mum, it's something you shouldn't mention
What did I get?
I got a detention

So don't follow the bad example that I've set you
Or you'll end up with a detention too
What will you get?
You'll get a detention

Cool Addiction

My head is stuck inside this book
I only meant to take a look
Till I saw what had been written
Instantly my mind was smitten
In a land of fascination
Sparking my imagination
Passions burning like a flame
Pictures dancing in my brain

My head is stuck inside this book
Just one page was all it took
I was focused and engaged
Thrilled, enthralled and entertained
Title, cover — so inviting
Words speak to me — so exciting
Such adventure, such intrigue
In a world of make believe

My head is stuck inside this book
Superglued, completely hooked
Unaware of all around me
Once this magic story found me
Characters feel like my friends
Plot unfolding till the end
Whether fact or whether fiction
Reading is a cool addiction

Fire Alarm

Beep, beep, beep, beep
'Pens down, books down'
Beep, beep, beep, beep
'March to the playground'

Beep, beep, beep, beep
'Leave bags, coats, hats'
Beep, beep, beep, beep
'Form a queue, don't chat'

Beep, beep, beep, beep
'Walk down the corridor'
Beep, beep, beep, beep
'Walk down the back stairs'

Beep, beep, beep, beep
'By the gate - two rows'
Beep, beep, beep, beep
'Just a drill? Who knows?'

Beep, beep, beep, beep
'Answer when your name's called'
Beep, beep, beep, beep
'Jayden — drop the football!'

Beep, beep, beep, beep
'Anyone seen Charlotte?'
Beep, beep, beep, beep
'She's stuck in the toilet!'

Beep, beep, beep, beep
'Wait and wait and wait and wait'
Beep, beep, beep, beep
'Dinner time will be late'

Beep, beep, beep, beep
'The fire brigade's in school'
Beep, beep, beep, beep
'No fire found at all'

Beep, beep, beep, beep
'Walk up the back stairs'
Beep, beep, beep, beep
'Walk up the corridor'

Beep, beep, beep, beep
Teacher said 'Two out of ten'
Beep, beep, beep, beep
'Tomorrow we will try again'

Beep, beep, beep, beep...

Have a Laugh

Have a chuckle
Have a giggle
Till your belly bobs and jiggles
Go on — act completely daft
Have a laugh
Ha! Ha! Ha!

You'll feel jolly
You'll feel cheery
When your day is dull and dreary
Don't sing in your shower or bath
Have a laugh
Ha! Ha! Ha!

Ha! Ha! Ha!
He! He! He!
Try a bit of comedy
Laugh, laugh, laugh
Have a laugh!
Ha! Ha! Ha!

Make a smirk
Make a smile
Keep on grinning all the while
Like hyenas, not giraffes
Have a laugh
Ha! Ha! Ha!

Why be grumpy?
Why be moody?
When you're down and bored and broody
Reach out to your happy half
Have a laugh
Ha! Ha! Ha!

Ha! Ha! Ha!
He! He! He!
Melt away your misery
Laugh, laugh, laugh
Have a laugh!
Ha! Ha! Ha!

Ha! Ha! Ha!
He! He! He!
Read some funny poetry
Laugh, laugh, laugh
Have a laugh!
Ha! Ha! Ha!

My Dad Thinks He's Cool

My Dad thinks he's cool
But he's not cool at all
He embarrasses me at the school gate
Attempting to speak street slang to all of my mates
Dad — you're not eleven, you've turned 38

My Dad thinks he's cool
But he's not cool at all
It's ever so painful when he sings along
To all of my latest favourite songs
He whines out of tune getting all the words wrong

My Dad thinks he's cool
But he's not cool at all
He wears new fashions to try and impress
Though under his shirt you'll see a string vest
He'd score a big fat zero in the `How Cool R U?' test

My Dad thinks he's cool
But he's not cool at all
He tries to play football with the rest of my team
His skills on the pitch are the worst I've ever seen
Out-tackled and out-dribbled by kids of thirteen

My Dad thinks he's cool
But he's not cool at all
So he'll never beat me at computer gaming
Despite hours and hours of meticulous training
I'm beating all records while he's doing my brain in

My Dad thinks he's cool
But he's not cool at all
And if you're reading this Dad
I hope you understand
Why I'd like all these mad things you do to be banned
I love you as you are so, please — act like a man!

My Dad thinks he's cool
But he's not cool at all

Match of the Day

We hide under the table
We cower behind the chair
We hear words that we've never heard
As swearing fills the air

The TV screen's been damaged
The remote control's been mashed
The living room's a battlefield
The furniture's been trashed

Dad's blood pressure is rising
Mum tells him 'Please, calm down!'
Blue veins are bulging from his head
His heart begins to pound

While steam pours out his nostrils
His feet stamp on the floor
A hundred crazed gorillas
Would shrivel at his roar

There's dinner on the carpet
There's beer spilt down his jeans
He turns a shade of purple
Yellow, orange, red and green

He writhes around in agony
Yells, 'I can't take no more!'
Though I thought sport was just for fun
To him it's just for war

Our windows are all broken
Our satellite dish is smashed
All extremely annoying
But Dad's way of enjoying
Another England football match

When I am Prime Minister

When I am Prime Minister
You'll have homework by the tonne
Maths lessons will quadruple
I'll fine you for having fun

In the Tower of London dungeon
I'll imprison the royalty
On pound coin heads you'll find me instead
All kids will be forced to eat greens

At my residence, 10 Downing Street
I'll rest with my feet up
While passing laws guaranteeing for sure
Just my team can win the Cup

Those nations I find annoying
My armies will invade in a flash
Then march their way round to your house
To confiscate your cash

Your screensavers and wallpapers
Will have to bear my face
Holidays and birthdays too
Will vanish without a trace

My special police will steal your sweets
Toys, TVs, books and games
I'll tax anyone who speaks or laughs
Or dares to misspell my name

Each weekday you'll hear only classical music
Only opera at the weekends
These are the things I promise to do
When I become PM

With my hand holding the master switch
I'll control the entire country
So tell me, next time there's an election, please
Will you be voting for me?

Orangutan, utan, utan, utan, utan, utan

Who's swinging on that tree
Eats fruit and veg for tea?
The orange one who's lots of fun and children queue to see

Orangutan, utan, utan, utan, utan, utan
Orangutan, utan, utan, utan, utan, utan

With arms extremely long
Huge muscles, super-strong
He says his second cousin's the gorilla called King Kong

Orangutan, utan, utan, utan, utan, utan
Orangutan, utan, utan, utan, utan, utan

He's jumping up and down
Fists thumping on the ground
He loves to play so every day he's monkeying around

Orangutan, utan, utan, utan, utan, utan
Orangutan, utan, utan, utan, utan, utan

His home is way out east
The cleverest of beasts
He picks his nose, he bites his toes, then scratches all his fleas

Orangutan, utan, utan, utan, utan, utan
Orangutan, utan, utan, utan, utan, utan

He likes to beat his chest
Tries so hard to impress

Of all the apes you've ever met who'd you think is the best?

Orangutan, utan, utan, utan, utan, utan
Orangutan, utan, utan, utan, utan, utan

Orangutan, utan, utan, utan, utan, utan
Orangutan, utan, utan, utan, utan, utan

Mr Teacher is Our Teacher

Mr Teacher is our teacher
'It's tricky to explain'
He told us when he taught us
Then he told us once again

'I'm your teacher, Mr Teacher
'You say "teacher" twice
'I was born a Teacher
'Been a Teacher all my life'

Mr Teacher is our teacher
It messes with our brains
Though teacher is the job he does
It's also his last name

He's married to a teacher
So she's called 'Teacher' too
Mrs Teacher is a teacher
Also teaching at our school

They've got two Teacher children
Who may grow up to teach
A total of four Teachers teaching
Would be really neat!

But now we're even more confused
'Cause Mr Teacher said
'A new Headteacher starts tomorrow...
'And her name's "Mrs Head"!'

The Invisible Lady

I'm going out with the Invisible Lady
I'm meeting her for a date
I'm going out with the Invisible Lady
She said she'd meet me at eight
But she's making me wait
She's one hour late
Though I couldn't find her
If I was standing behind her

I'm going out with the Invisible Lady
Though what she looks like I don't know
I'm going out with the Invisible Lady
I could so easily tread on her toe
Or leave without her when we go
To the cinema or to a show
It is quite apparent
She's totally transparent

I'm going out with the Invisible Lady
I walked right through her last night
I'm going out with the Invisible Lady
I can't see her though it's broad daylight
Like a polar bear on a background of white
She's out of my sight
The torture I've been through
'Cause my girlfriend's see-through

I'm going out with the Invisible Lady
Though we've never met face to face
I'm going out with the Invisible Lady
She could be standing in this very place
Though all you see is empty space
Don't say I'm a nutcase!
My woman's invisible — it's true
She just vanishes into the blue

I'm going out with the Invisible Lady
I'm still waiting here on my own
I'm going out with the Invisible Lady
Looks like one more evening alone
She's got no skin and bones
But she still could have phoned
I guess I'm not in her future plans
Perhaps she's run off — with the Invisible Man

My Superpower

My mate Max has laser vision
Melting metal with perfect precision
Browning toast and the Sunday roast
Who has his own show on television?
My mate Max who has laser vision

My cousin Khadija can teleport
Changing location with a single thought
In the blink of an eye, England to Dubai
Who moves from country to country without a passport?
My cousin Khadija who can teleport

My buddy Ben can shrink to ant-size
When he does, you can never fail to be surprised
Though possessing human strength
at one millimetre in length
Who still has to be wary of hungry flies?
My buddy Ben who can shrink to ant-size

My pal Priya is telekinetic
She can move any object by looking at it
Shifting a fridge, lifting a bridge
Who do all my class call 'totally terrific'?
My pal Priya who is telekinetic

My sister Sara can change her shape
Yesterday an octopus, today an ape
The queen of disguise, often hard to recognise
Who morphs from a camel into a snake?
My sister Sara who can change her shape

But I can't turn invisible, run extra fast or fly
As a poet I thought 'I'm just an ordinary guy'
Then I saw I could inspire, excite, engage
Make people listen, read, turn over a page
Unlock creativity, spark imagination
Master the skill of communication

So, if you want a superpower too
Whether you're a girl or guy
Get typing, get writing
And give poetry a try

Terrific Tot

He's a hero in a nappy
But don't let that put you off
He can tackle twenty rhinos
He can handle rough and tough
Though he nearly is a newborn
And still peeing in a pot
He's a baby trained to save me
Shout his name
Terrific Tot!

Special milk gives him his power
Special biscuits give him speed
Holds his rattle during battle
Always back for his next feed
Hear him goo-goo, hear him gaa-gaa
While his nose is dripping snot
He's the one the needy run to
Shout his name
Terrific Tot!

Spot him in his bib of spandex
Matching mittens on his hands
Grabbing kids from burning buildings
Crushing evil where it stands
Very tiny, sometimes whiny
Spending nighttimes in a cot
He's a cutie dressed in booties
Shout his name
Terrific Tot!

Often absent from his nursery
Missing sessions to fight crime
Tightly cuddling his teddy
Catching villains every time
Watch him sucking on his dummy
As his mummy wipes his bot
Who's the best to stage a rescue?
Shout his name
Terrific Tot!

Underneath the Mask

Underneath the mask I'm a regular guy
Underneath the mask I'm quiet and shy
Underneath the mask I'm human too
Underneath the mask I'm just like you

I've a life that's ordinary
I go shopping and watch telly

Underneath the mask I'm much more humble
Underneath the mask I'm vulnerable
Underneath the mask I'm not well known
Underneath the mask I'm all alone

I get nervous when I'm flying
When I fight I'm scared of dying

Underneath the mask I'm not so strong
Underneath the mask my powers have gone
Underneath the mask is a different man
Underneath the mask is who I really am

Nobody will recognise me hidden by my secret ID
There's no superhero to see underneath the mask

Kids Love Ketchup

Kids love ketchup on their chips
Kids love ketchup on their crisps
Kids love ketchup on their eggs
Kids love ketchup on their bread

Kids love ketchup on baked beans
And to drown the taste of greens
Kids love ketchup, though of course
Posh kids say 'tomato sauce'

Kids love ketchup on pork chops
Chicken, chocolate, lollipops
Kids love ketchup, they form queues
Just to watch that ketchup ooooooooooze

Kids love ketchup on meat pies
Make my bottle jumbo size
Kids love ketchup on their plates
It's the relish they most rate

Kids love ketchup on their hair
Hands, nose, clothes and everywhere
Kids love ketchup twenty-four seven
Like to live in ketchup heaven

Kids love ketchup on their cheese
Kids love ketchup freshly squeeeeeeeeeezed
Dig the red ketchuppy mess
Do kids love ketchup?
Yes! Yes! Yes!

Pizza Delivery Man

Pizza delivery man
Pizza delivery man

I'm the man to bring your pizza
It's my job, it's my career

Pizza delivery man
Pizza delivery man

Mushroom, onion, chicken topping
Ham, tomato, there's no stopping

Pizza delivery man
Pizza delivery man

Mega size with pepperoni
You can order if you phone me

Pizza delivery man
Pizza delivery man

Love to taste that mozzarella?
Look no further I'm your fella

Pizza delivery man
Pizza delivery man

Parsley, basil, oregano
You'll believe you're in Milano

Pizza delivery man
Pizza delivery man

Garlic bread I'm baking also
Pick your dinner from my menu

Pizza delivery man
Pizza delivery man

To your door in half an hour
Brought to you by pizza power

Pizza delivery man
Pizza delivery man

Pizza delivery man
Pizza delivery man

My Secret Chocolate Stash

I've got a secret chocolate stash
That's hidden in my house
It's stored securely somewhere safe
For when my sweets run out

It's buried under lock and key
And is completely mine
A scrumptious bar of heaven
My emergency supply

And if today is grim and grey
With rain instead of sun
I'll bolt my door, sit on my floor
Then stuff my face for fun

I know it isn't healthy
I know it isn't right
But I just can't resist a food
So beautiful to bite

Twelve perfect squares to savour
Gobble, nibble, nosh and pick
I don't care that I've eaten dinner
And am feeling sick

Who is the one to turn to
When I am feeling down?
My friendly, fatty, sugary mate
Delicious, smooth and brown

You can turn my bedroom inside out
Until it's totally trashed
Still you'll never, ever, ever find...
My secret chocolate stash

Claude le Croissant

Je m'appelle Claude le Croissant
The alternative to bread
Why bore yourself with sandwiches?
Just purchase me instead

Je m'appelle Claude le Croissant
For your breakfast, lunch or tea
My body shape's a crescent moon
Or like the letter 'c'

You can stuff me with a salad
You can eat me with cheese spread
You can sprinkle me with almonds
Then shake sugar on my head
I have travelled here by Eurostar
From somewhere near the Med

Je m'appelle Claude le Croissant
I am neither bun nor cake
Soft and flaky I'm the pastry
That's the tastiest of bakes

Je m'appelle Claude le Croissant
I'm the favoured food of France
Other doughs try to outdo me
But they never stand a chance

You can cover me with butter
You can smother me with jam
You can serve me with salami
You can fill me up with ham
Your companion from the Continent
Remember who I am

Je m'appelle Claude le Croissant
Star of your patisserie
If you bite me and you like me
Shout out 'Oui! Oui! Oui!'

Hot Stuff

There's a hole in the plate
A hole in the mat
A hole in the table
Scorched fur on the cat

My trousers are burning
My throat is ablaze
The pot used for cooking
Now disintegrates

A hole's in the carpet
And on the stone floor
A window has blown out
We've lost the front door

The fire brigade's coming
The flames can't be stopped
'Cause Mum's piri-piri chicken was...
Hot! Hot! Hot!

The Rhyme Thief

Watch out for the Rhyme Thief
She is bound to steal your rhyme
If you try to make one
She will take it every...

Beware this wicked woman
Who is ruining this poem
Where is she likely next to strike?
We have no way of...

She sees it as a challenge
She sees it as a game
Collecting all the words we're using
When they sound the...

You'll know when she has visited
You'll find an empty space
Once there was a rhyme
But there's a gap now in its...

Your verses, raps and odes
Should be hidden from her sight
Mind your back, she might attack
As you sit down to...

Stop this ghastly supervillain
Burglar and crook
Replace the rhymes she's stolen
And don't let her spoil this...

Mwahahahaha!

To defeat superheroes
Is a difficult thing
You could use nasty weapons
Plot and plan deadly schemes
You may mix poison potions
Build a laser-powered car
But you must emit an evil laugh
Mwahahahaha!

You might wear flashy costumes
Build a robotic brain
Hold a planet to ransom
Have a spine-chilling name
Forge a lasting alliance
With a warlord from Mars
But you must express an evil laugh
Mwahahahaha!

You can strengthen your muscles
Gain the power of flight
Or become an immortal
So you never will die
Maybe form your own army
And destroy a distant star
But you must unleash an evil laugh
Mwahahahaha!

It's important, essential
It's a tool of the trade
As without it you'll struggle
Score the lowest of grades
You should practise then practise
Practise, practise really hard
Until you possess an evil laugh
Mwahahahaha!

Paintball

Paintball
A truly terrible teen
The most colourful villain you've ever seen
A rainbow explosion
On the attack
Red, orange, yellow, green, blue
SPLAT!

Paintball
Creates a collage of crime
Dressed in glittering pink and luminous lime
Sneaking in shadows
Paint gun attached
Red, orange, yellow, green, blue
SPLAT!

Paintball
Beware her spectrum of sin
Doing exactly what it says on her tin
Acrylic or oil
Gloss, silk or matt
Red, orange, yellow, green, blue
SPLAT!

Paintball
Playing a dangerous game
She'll stop you, rob you then graffiti her name
A poisonous palette
So watch your back
Red, orange, yellow, green, blue
SPLAT!
SPLAT!
SPLAT!
SPLAT!
SPLAT!

Chicken in the Kitchen

There's a chicken in the kitchen
There's a bat on my hat
There's a bee in my tea
There's a flea on the cat

There's a gibbon in the garage
There's a possum in the park
There's a crab in the lab
There's a moose marooned on Sark

There's a frog on a log
(With a hog and a dog)
There's a rhino on the lino
There's a badger in a bog

There's a prawn on the lawn
There's a caiman in a cake
There's a hamster in my hair
There's a lizard in the lake

There's a turkey in the toilet
There's a heron in the hall
But where's the dodo gone to
'Cause I can't find him at all?

Tarantula Down Your Toilet

I'm the tarantula down your toilet
Your prowler in the pan
I want to bite and frighten you
Whatever way I can
I'll nibble on your bottom
I'll stalk you on your seat
'Cause yes you've guessed that human flesh
Is what I love to eat

I'm the tarantula down your toilet
I've chosen here as home
Don't linger on the loo too long
While playing with your phone
For when I'm feeling hungry
My fangs will make their mark
You'd better switch the light on
If you enter after dark

I'm the tarantula down your toilet
You'll hear me splash about
Prod me, poke me, push me
But I'm never moving out
I could live in your cupboard
Your kitchen, loft or shed
Yet in this bowl is where I roll
And where I've made my bed

I'm the tarantula down your toilet
Who's causing you dismay
Don't get ideas to calm your fears
By flushing me away
My kingdom is your bathroom
Where I can wander free
So pick a new location
When you have the need to pee

We Want the Quagga!

(The quagga was a species of zebra, last seen at the end of the 1800s)

We want the quagga!
We want the quagga back
We miss his stripes of brown and white
He vanished just like that

We want the quagga!
Why did he disappear?
He seemed such fun and hurt no one
He's not been seen in years

We want the quagga!
Where did he wander to?
You won't spot him in Senegal
New Zealand or Peru

We want the quagga!
From South African plains
He'd quag and trot, chew grass a lot
And shake his shaggy mane

We want the quagga!
No longer found in zoos
Although of course, quite like a horse
A substitute won't do

We want the quagga!
So sadly hunted down
First he was chased and then erased
Or moved to out of town

We want the quagga!
We love bears, wolves and yaks
Cows, camels, goats, aardvarks and stoats
But want the quagga back!

I'm an Electric Eel

I'm an electric eel
Delivering shocks
An electric eel
Blowing off your socks

An electric eel
Giving you a jolt
An electric eel
Can you feel my volts?

I hang out in river beds
Touch me you might end up dead

I'm an electric eel
Even scaring sharks
An electric eel
Glowing in the dark

An electric eel
Don't eat me with chips
An electric eel
I will burn your lips

Slimy, smooth and slippery
Full of electricity

I'm an electric eel
Long and sleek and slim
An electric eel
See me splash and swim

An electric eel
With no arms or legs
An electric eel
Which end is my head?

Run on mains or battery
Looks like someone's flattened me

I'm an electric eel
Such a powerful chap
An electric eel
With a zap, zap
ZZZZZZZZZZZAP!

Animal Football Premiership Table

1. BEARmingham City
2. NEWTcastle Utd
3. Queen's Park REINDEERS
4. West HAMSTER Utd
5. BarceLIONa
6. MANXchester City
7. Tottenham OCELOTspur
8. Sheffield HENSday
9. BLACKBIRD Rovers
10. STOAT City
11. Aston GORILLA (previously known as Aston CHINCHILLA)
12. FuLAMB
13. LiverPOODLE
14. WASPford
15. DerBEE County
16. Brighton & DOVE Albion
17. SWANsea City
18. ChelSEAL
19. Real MaSQUID

And, of course

20. WOLVES

Good Morning!

Good morning Daniel
'Here Sir!'
Good morning Colette
'I'm NOT here Sir!'
Good morning Aaron
'Bonjour monsieur!'
Good morning Darshan
'Ill with chicken pox Sir!'
Good morning Fiona
'Still in Australia Sir!'
Good morning Victoria
'I am present, in attendance and ready to work extremely hard Sir!'
Good morning Heema
'Just been sick Sir!'
Good morning Rosa
'Konnichiwa Sir!'
Wake up Lena...
'Zzzzzzzzzzzzzzz'
Good morning Marco
'Morning Miss!'
Good morning Joe F
'Hola, buenos días!'

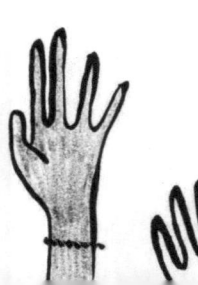

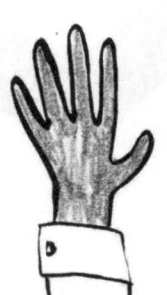

Good morning Joe P
'Been kidnapped by aliens Sir!'
Good morning Precious
'Aye, aye Captain!'
Good morning Olivia
'Not back from last Christmas Sir!'
Good afternoon Rafael
'Late again Sir!'
Good morning Sid
'Yabba dabba doo Sir!'
Good morning Talia
'Aaaaaaaaaachooooooo!'
Good morning Gabby
'Thank you and I hope you have a very good morning too Sir'
Good morning Maya
'Sir morning good! Today backwards talking I'm!'
Good morning Eric
'Hello Dad!'
Good morning Neal
Good morning Neal
GOOD MORNING NEAL ZETTER!
'Sorry Sir...I'm busy writing this poem about you calling the register!'

Blah! Blah! Blah!

Dad goes on about politics
And when he plans to clean his car
Complains about the economy
But all I hear is
'Blah! Blah! Blah!'

Mum moans about the mortgage
Counts calories in her chocolate bar
Asks me to tidy my room again
But all I hear is
'Blah! Blah! Blah!'

Grandpa retells us war stories
Explains how he first met Grandma
Groans about his rheumatism
But all I hear is
'Blah! Blah! Blah!'

Auntie criticises my clothes
Says I look like I'm from Mars
Insists in her day everything was better
But all I hear is
'Blah! Blah! Blah!'

If only they'd talk about what interests me
Television, football, movie stars
Superheroes, school, books, music
But all I hear is
'Blah! Blah! Blah!'

'Blah! Blah! Blah!'
'Blah! Blah! Blah!'
All I hear from adults is
'Blah! Blah! Blah!'

Mum and Dad are Kissing Again

Mum and Dad are kissing again
I'm too embarrassed to look
Mum and Dad are kissing again
My head hides in a book

Mum and Dad are kissing again
Though all my friends are round
Mum and Dad are kissing again
Make squishy kissy sounds

They kiss at the dinner table
They kiss watching TV
They kiss in the kitchen
They kiss on the settee

Mum and Dad are kissing again
Both puckering their lips
Mum and Dad are kissing again
I think I'm feeling sick

Mum and Dad are kissing again
Two lovebirds in a cage
Mum and Dad are kissing again
I wish they'd act their age

They kiss in the street
They kiss in the shops
They kiss in the garden
They kiss around the clock

Mum and Dad are kissing again
Such passion should be banned
Mum and Dad are kissing again
Why can't they just shake hands?

Mum and Dad are kissing again
Like Hollywood movie stars
Mum and Dad are kissing again
Mwah!
Mwah!
Mwah!

My Me-Only Zone

This is my bedroom
My door's always locked
I won't let you in though you
Knock! Knock! Knock!

It's my den, my hideout
It's my special place
I'm warning you — keep out of my personal space!
With stickers and photos
And posters on walls
This is my territory where I make the rules

This is my bedroom
My door's always locked
I won't let you in though you
Knock! Knock! Knock!

That name on the sign's
Not belonging to you
Here I play my music, computer games too
No adults may enter
They're outlawed, they're banned
While I speak a language they don't understand

This is my bedroom
My door's always locked
I won't let you in though you
Knock! Knock! Knock!

I chose my own carpet
My curtains, my quilt
So I don't need Jack – it's the room that I built
I watch my TV
Then I chat on my phone
'Cause this is my magical Me-Only Zone

This is my bedroom
My door's always locked
I won't let you in though you
Knock! Knock! Knock!

I won't let you in though you
Knock! Knock! Knock!

Fake News

The Great Fire of London began in McDonald's
The Battle of Hastings was fought in 1994
Queen Victoria was the first person on the Moon
It was Batman who started the Second World War

Cavemen created computer games
The Vikings drove around in cars
William Shakespeare wrote only nursery rhymes
In 1985 Earth was invaded by Mars

Elvis Presley was the third US President
Dinosaurs became extinct in 2003
Florence Nightingale invented television
And I failed all my exams in history

Haunted House

There are werewolves in the living room who
Howl! Howl! HOWL!
There are beasties in the bathroom hear them
Growl! Growl! GROWL!

In the graveyard lurk the zombies not quite
Dead! Dead! DEAD!
If you're passing through be careful where you
Tread! Tread TREAD!

Mummies resting in their coffins rattle
Chains! Chains! CHAINS!
In the kitchen ghosts and ghouls are baking
Brains! Brains! BRAINS!

In the dining room a vampire's drinking
Blood! Blood! BLOOD!
Poltergeists prowl in the basement banging
Thud! Thud! THUD!

Wicked wizards in the tower weave their
Spells! Spells! SPELLS!
Evil witches mix their stinky potion
Smells! Smells! SMELLS!

And the belfry's full of freaky flapping
Bats! Bats! BATS!
While the sewers run with scary squeaky
Rats! Rats! RATS!

Spiders hang upon the rooftop spinning
Webs! Webs! WEBS!
From the stairwell slime is dripping on your
Head! Head! HEAD!

Now a storm cloud is erupting with a
Crack! Crack! CRACK!
So I'm leaving in a hurry won't be
Back! Back! BACK!

I Don't Like Sssssnakes

The way they feel, the way they bite
The way they curl up very tight
The way they slither 'cross the ground
The way they slide without a sound
I don't...
Like...
Sssssnakes

The way their tongues are shaped like forks
The way they never smile or talk
The way they have no hair at all
The way they cannot kick a ball
I don't...
Like...
Sssssnakes

The way they're still until they strike
The way they're rubbish riding bikes
The way there's poison in their fangs
The way they hang about in gangs
I don't...
Like...
Ssssssnakes

The way they shed their scaly skin
The way they look so long and thin
The way they hide inside your bed
The way they might prefer me dead
I don't...
Like...
Sssssssnakes

Cobra, rattlesnake or adder
Grass snake, python or black mamba
Boa constrictor or sidewinder
Anaconda or pit viper
I don't...
Like...
Sssssssssssssnakessssssssssssss!

My Mummy is a Mummy

My mummy is a mummy linen-wrapped from toe to head
She sleeps in a sarcophagus instead of in a bed
She's not keen on the daytime 'cause she's frightened of the light
The bits of her you'd recognise are hidden out of sight

While most of us use bandages for grazes and for cuts
She uses them for fashion and I think that's pretty nuts
Her fondness for Egyptian culture cannot be denied
Last week she bought a pyramid and made her home inside

My mummy is a mummy — it's incredible yet true
She hopes to meet the pharaohs, sphinx and Cleopatra too
It's very complicated when she's taking baths or showers
Her skin's a mess and getting dressed can take her several hours

Though Mum says that it didn't hurt when she was first embalmed
She often finds it difficult to move her legs and arms
I shouted, 'Dad, this is so mad and also it's not right'
But he's not fussed 'cause he becomes a werewolf every night!

Something Down the Plughole

There's something down the plughole
There's something down the sink
I felt a claw and saw a paw
While at the tap to drink

A weird and eerie creature
Composed of sludge and slime
It crawled up from the sewage pipe
And feeds on grease and grime

Emitting awful odours
It hasn't got a name
The Beastie from the Basin?
The Demon from the Drain?

Who knows if it is friendly
Or if it might attack?
Be careful when you're washing up
In case it wants a snack!

We pushed it with a plunger
We poked it with a knife
But still it stays, won't go away
The lurker in our pipe

We're hearing burps at midnight
We're hearing slurps at dawn
So enter our kitchen at your own risk
Don't say you've not been warned...

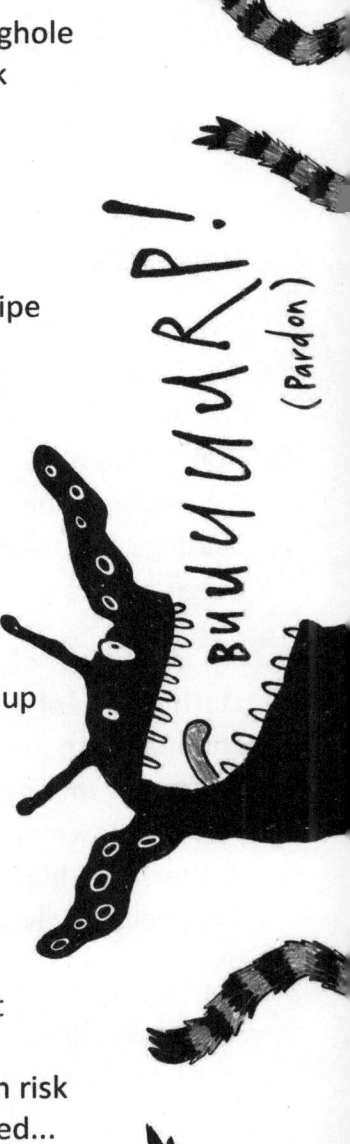

BuuuuuRP! (Pardon)

Scared?

I'm not scared of...
Creepy hairy caterpillars
Chest-beating escaped gorillas
Telling people I've been crying
Or my Uncle David dying
Mister Rankle (shouty teacher)
'Zombie Doomsday' (horror feature)

I'm not scared of...
Prickly spiky falling conkers
Towering trees like massive monsters
Bonfire Night's exploding rockets
Finding squashed slugs in my pockets
Skating on the ice in winter
Digging out a wooden splinter

I'm not scared of...
Starting school on Monday morning
Thunder with no lightning warning
Heights of mountains, depths of valleys
Walking down deserted alleys
Bothersome big boils and blisters
Cinderella's ugly sisters

But I am scared of when I can no longer pretend
And must admit that I'm scared
To all my family and friends

BONUS POEMS

Things That Can't Fit in My Shoe

Dinosaur
Aberdeen
Ice-cream van
Time machine
Lawnmower
Cowboy hat
Chicken shop
Next-door's cat

Apple tree
Traffic light
Battleship
Building site
Jupiter
London Bridge
Bowling ball
My Nan's fridge

Saxophone
Double bed
Motorbike
Someone's head
Wheelie bin
Kangaroo
None of these fit in my shoe

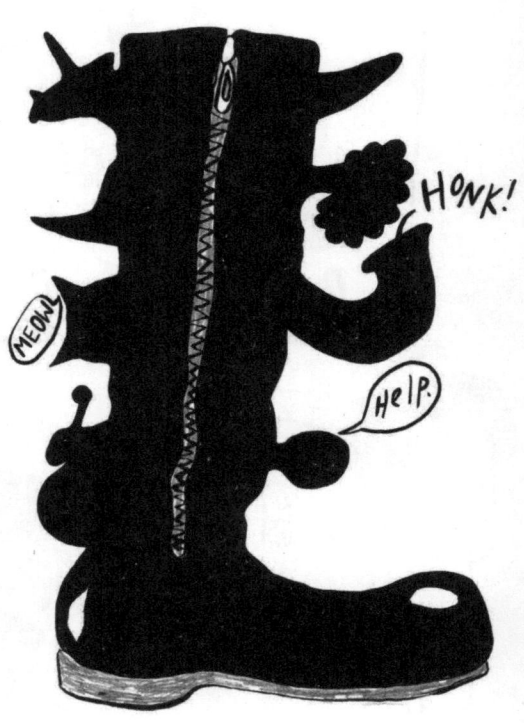

Just Be You

It's the smile on your face
It's the curls in your hair
It's the spark in your eye
It's the clothes that you wear

It's the food that you eat
It's the room where you sleep
It's the games that you play
It's the friends that you keep

It's the songs that you love
It's the books that you read
It's the dreams that you have
All your wants and your needs

It's the words that you speak
It's the things that you do
So why be someone else?
Just be you

About the Poet

Neal Zetter began writing poetry when he was six years old. Since 1994, he has staged his fun poetry-writing workshops and performances in hundreds of schools and libraries in the UK and beyond, teaching 3-to-103-year-olds to create their own fantastic poems.

He has won the Silver Book Award, been acclaimed by the Reading Agency and Book Trust, had poems on London's buses, in the Guardian newspaper and in many anthologies. He has performed his adult poems on radio, in the Royal Festival Hall, at a League 2 football match, festivals, weddings and funerals (really) and countless West End comedy clubs. He also hosted his own club for ten years.

This is Neal's 13th book and his 11th for Troika. For all things Neal see cccpworkshops.co.uk

About the Illustrator

Emily Ford is a freelance illustrator from Cumbria. From a young age she had a passion for storytelling and reading, which inspired her to create her own imaginary worlds populated with characters and magic. After studying for a degree in illustration, she began working on children's books inspired by classic fairy tales and comics. Emily collaborated with her friend Stevie Westgarth to create Troika's *Aife and Stray: Seven Style Secrets for a Perilous Party*. She has illustrated *Riding a Lion* by Coral Rumble for Troika and Neal Zetter's *When the Bell Goes,* published in 2021.

About this Collection

In this rollicking greatest-hits collection covering Neal's first eight Troika books, he has chosen poems that children have most frequently requested during his twenty years of school visits. Books covered include *Bees in My Bananas, It's Not Fine to Sit on a Porcupine, Here Come the Superheroes, Yuck and Yum, Invasion of the Supervillains, Gorilla Ballerina, When the Bell Goes* and *Scared?*. With the inclusion of two new bonus poems, this is a fantastic introduction to the ever-creative mind of one of the UK's most beloved children's poets.

troika

The home of great children's books

Troika is a small independent children's book publisher. We're based in the UK.

Follow us on social media

 @troikabooks

 @TroikaBooks